Termites on a Stick

A Chimp Learns to Use a Tool

By Michèle Coxon

STAR BRIGHT BOOKS

NEW YORK

To my darling mum, Peggy Bootle,
for always being there for us and the grandchildren.
All my love. —M.C.

Published in the United States of America by Star Bright Books, Inc., New York.
The name Star Bright Books and the Star Bright Books logo are registered
trademarks of Star Bright Books, Inc. Please visit www.starbrightbooks.com.

ISBN-13: 978-1-59572-121-1

Printed in China (WKT) 9 8 7 6 5 4 3 2 1

Library of Congress Cataloging-in-Publication Data

Coxon, Michèle.
  Termites on a stick : a chimp learns to use a tool / by Michèle Coxon.
      p. cm.
  ISBN 978-1-59572-121-1
  1. Chimpanzees--Behavior--Juvenile literature. 2. Tool use in animals--Juvenile literature.
I. Title.
  QL737.P96C69 2007
  599.885'15--dc22
                        2007034324

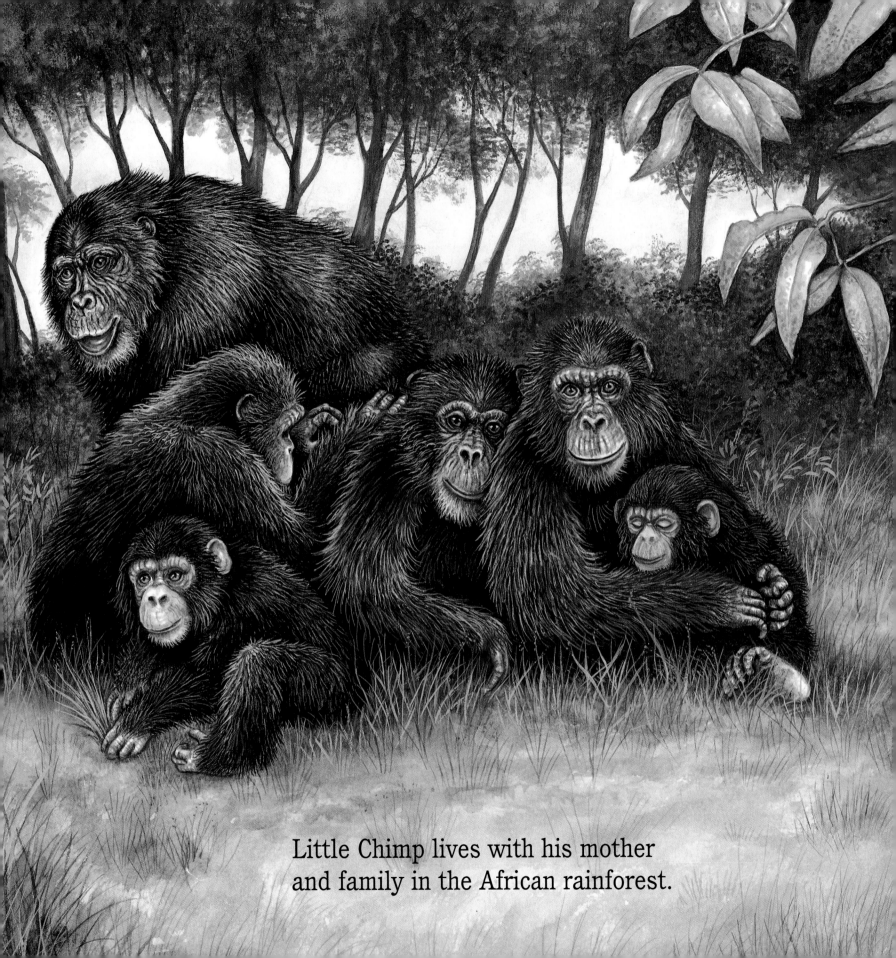

Little Chimp lives with his mother
and family in the African rainforest.

He loves to swing in the trees and roll
around on the ground with his friends.

Little Chimp sometimes plays with his baboon friend, but if he gets too rough, mother baboon gets angry.

Little Chimp runs to his mother for protection.
She grooms him, which comforts him and also
keeps him clean.

When Little Chimp gets hungry, he likes to eat fruits and leaves and also insects. His mother has spotted a large group of mounds. They are termite nests!

Termites are his mother's favorite snack.
She finds a small branch and breaks it off a tree.

She pulls the leaves off the branch to make the stick smooth. Little Chimp watches her closely. His mother carefully pushes the stick into a hole in one of the nests and fishes for termites.

When his mother pulls out the stick,
it is covered with juicy termites.

Little Chimp wants some, but his mother wants
him to learn to fish for termites on his own.

Little Chimp looks for a stick and he finds one on the ground. But when he tries to put it in the termite hole, it won't fit. It is too thick.

Little Chimp looks for another stick and finds one on the ground. But when he tries to put it in the termite hole, it breaks. It is too thin.

Little Chimp wonders what he can do. He climbs a tree and looks for another stick. He finds a small branch and breaks it off the tree.

Little Chimp remembers what his mother did. He pulls the leaves off the branch. He puts it in the termite hole. It is just right! It is not too thick and not too thin.

When Little Chimp pulls out the stick, it is covered with juicy termites. They taste delicious!

He fishes for termites again and again.

He hears his mother calling for him.

The sun is setting
and it is time for bed.

Little Chimp's mother has
made a leafy bed in a tree.
He climbs up the tree to be with her.

It will soon be dark.
Little Chimp falls asleep
with his mother's arms
wrapped around him.

About chimpanzees:

Chimpanzees live in the tropical rainforests and wooded savannahs of central and western Africa.

They live in family groups of twenty to a hundred members.

Young chimps stay with their mothers for five or six years.

Chimps eat mainly fruits, young leaves, seeds, flowers, insects, honey, eggs, and sometimes small animals.

Chimps use tools, such as sticks for termite fishing, stones to crack open nuts, and grass and leaves to wipe their hands and even their bottoms.

If you see a chimp grinning, it means it is frightened, not happy.

As forests are cleared for farming or logging, chimps lose their homes. Many chimps are killed for food or captured. Scientists believe that if this continues, in twenty years there will be no chimps left in the wild.

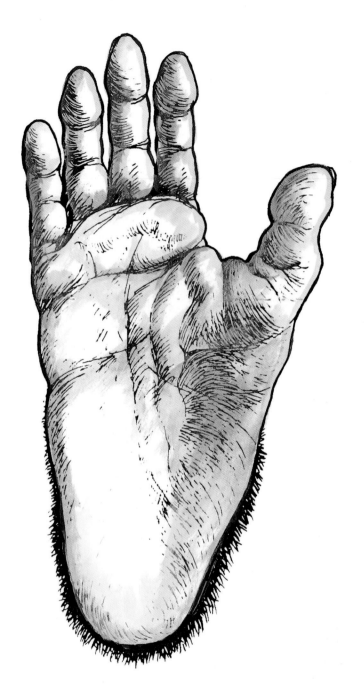

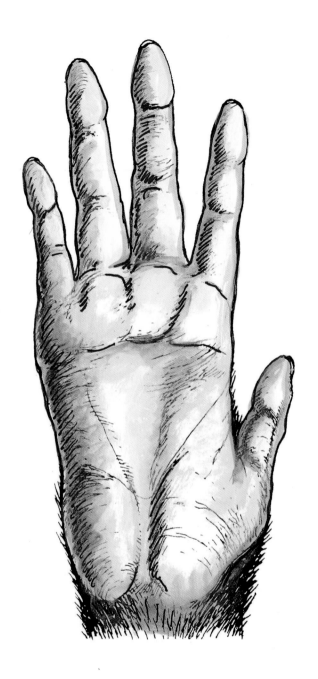

Chimps have feet like humans, but instead of big toes, they have prehensile thumbs. These help them use their feet like hands, so they can grip tree branches and climb really well.

Chimps also have hands like humans. They can perform precise movements such as plucking the thinnest leaves off a twig.

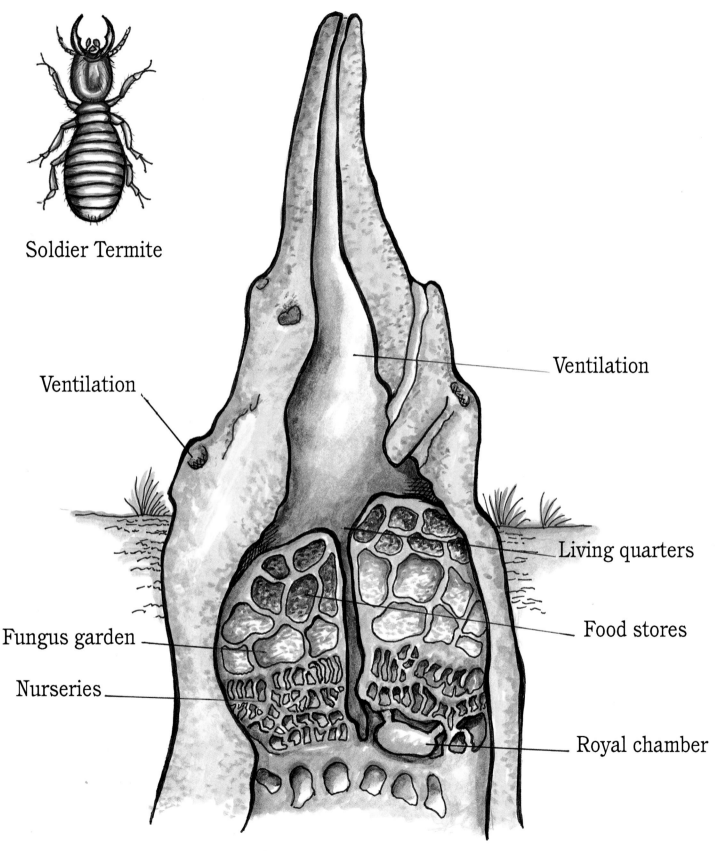

Soldier Termite

Ventilation

Ventilation

Living quarters

Fungus garden

Food stores

Nurseries

Royal chamber

Inside a termite's nest

How you can help save chimps:

Become a member of the Jane Goodall Institute. She has been studying these wonderful animals for over forty years.

Start or join a *Roots & Shoots* group in your school. *Roots & Shoots* is an environmental education program for young people from kindergarten through college.